Hank came up again in the fourth, and the first pitch was in the dirt. The boos started again. Then Downing threw a fast ball, right down the middle. Looking as relaxed as ever, Aaron snapped his wrists. The ball met the bat with a crack that could be heard throughout Atlanta Stadium. As the crowd screamed and cheered, the ball soared toward left center. It cleared the fence near the 385-foot sign and landed in the Braves' bullpen. It was Aaron's first swing of the game and his 715th home run. . . .

THE STORY OF HANK AARON
was originally published by
Julian Messner.

Critics' Corner:

"A biography illustrated by good action photographs. . . . Easy-to-read style and balanced coverage of personal and professional aspects of Aaron's life are strong points. A chart of Aaron's batting record is appended." —*Bulletin of the Center for Children's Books*, University of Chicago

"Above average as easy-to-read biographies go—especially those concerned with sports figures."
—*A.L.A. Booklist*

". . . contains all that a young reader will find relevant and the action pictures are truly professional and well chosen." —*Publishers Weekly*

About the Author:

BERNICE ELIZABETH YOUNG was a sports fan from the time she was a child and started going to Cleveland's Municipal Stadium on Saturday afternoons to watch the Cleveland Indians. In high school, Ms. Young played basketball and was also a regular referee following boys' rules. Writing for the *Glenville Torch,* her high-school newspaper, led to an invitation to a professional football game that sparked her love for the Cleveland Browns. Even after she moved to New York, Ms. Young continued to be a fan of the Browns and the Indians. Her favorite personalities in the world of sports include Tom Seaver, Larry Kenon and, naturally, the magnificent Hank Aaron. Ms. Young does freelance writing and is presently completing an historic study of her race's African ancestors. She has also written *The Picture Story of Frank Robinson.*

THE STORY OF
HANK AARON

(Original title: *The Picture Story of Hank Aaron*)

by B. E. YOUNG

Illustrated with photographs

AN ARCHWAY PAPERBACK
POCKET BOOKS · NEW YORK

THE STORY OF HANK AARON

Julian Messner edition published 1974

Archway Paperback edition published March, 1976

PICTURE CREDITS

United Press International: p. 13, 17, 19, 21, 33, 59, 69

Wide World Photos: p. iii, ix, 2, 5, 10-11, 14, 23, 28, 35, 37, 38, 39, 42, 43, 44-45, 46, 49, 50, 51, 52, 53, 54, 55, 56, 57, 60, 62, 64, 65, 67, 68, 70, 72-73, 74, 76, 78, 80

L

Published by
POCKET BOOKS, a division of Simon & Schuster, Inc.,
630 Fifth Avenue, New York, N.Y.

Archway Paperback editions are distributed in the U.S. by Simon & Schuster, Inc., 630 Fifth Avenue, New York, N.Y. 10020, and in Canada by Simon & Schuster of Canada, Ltd., Markham, Ontario, Canada.

1276

Standard Book Number: 671-29750-3.
Library of Congress Catalog Card Number: 73-19238.
This Archway Paperback edition is published by arrangement with Julian Messner. Copyright, ©, 1974, by Bernice Elizabeth Young. All rights reserved. *The Story of Hank Aaron* was originally published under the title *The Picture Story of Hank Aaron.* This book, or portions thereof, may not be reproduced by any means without permission of the original publisher: Julian Messner, a division of Simon & Schuster, Inc., 1 West 39th Street, New York, N.Y. 10018.
Printed in the U.S.A.

Sincere thanks to Patrick O'Brien, Dan Reimer and Jean-Jacques Rousseau for all their help and encouragement. Thanks also to Bob Hope of the Atlanta Braves for his kindness.

To George Michael Selizki—
Genius, Wizard and Prince

THE STORY OF
HANK AARON

On April 23, 1954, Henry Aaron hit his first home run as a major-league ballplayer. For the 20-year-old rookie, it was a dream come true.

Henry had loved baseball for as long as he could remember. While he was in grade school, he played baseball and softball almost every day. His interest in baseball came from his father.

Mr. Aaron worked as a boilermaker's helper for a ship-building company. But when he was young, he had been a semi-professional ballplayer. He taught Henry

1

Henry Aaron was 20 years old when he became a member of the Milwaukee Braves.

the game, and played with him whenever he could. Still, as much as Mr. Aaron enjoyed seeing Henry play baseball, he and Mrs. Aaron were more interested in having their son go to college.

Henry Louis Aaron was born on February 5, 1934, in Down the Bay, a run-down section of Mobile, Alabama. He was the third of seven children. While he was still very young, his family moved to Toulmanville, a nicer section of Mobile. Close to his new home was Hartwell Field, where major-league baseball teams played exhibition games on their way north after spring training. Henry loved to go to those games. So, to earn the money for a ticket, he took jobs after school. He mowed lawns and worked on an ice truck.

Henry's job on the ice truck was to deliver ice. In those days, most people still had iceboxes instead of electric refrigerators. In order to keep food cold, a block of ice was put into the icebox.

Using a sharp-pointed ice pick, Henry marked off a piece of ice the size the customer wanted. Then he chopped the piece

3

away from the huge cake of ice, which almost filled the back of the truck. With large, heavy tongs, he swung the 25- or 50-pound block of ice to his shoulder and carried it into the customer's kitchen. Some people say that Henry's work on the ice truck helped develop his great wrists.

With the money he earned, Henry saw such world champion teams as the Boston Red Sox and the New York Yankees, and famous players like Joe DiMaggio, Bobby Doerr, Eddie Stanky, and Mickey Owen. More important, one day at Hartwell Field he saw major-league baseball's first black player, Jackie Robinson. That was the day Henry made up his mind. He was going to be a baseball player like Robinson.

When Henry was 15, Ed Scott, a neighbor, asked if he would like to play with the Mobile Black Bears, a local semi-professional team. Henry was thrilled. But his mother was not. Mrs. Aaron wanted Henry to finish high school and go on to college. She felt that unless her son got a good education, he would have trouble finding a job that would pay him well.

4

At Hartwell Field in Mobile, Alabama, Henry Aaron first watched Dodger third baseman, Jackie Robinson. Robinson was the first black man to play on a major-league baseball team.

But Henry and Ed Scott would not give up. Mr. Scott explained that Henry would only be playing one day a week—on Sunday. He wouldn't have to miss school at all. And Henry would be making money—between $5 and $10 each time he played, depending on how many people came to watch the game.

Finally, Mrs. Aaron gave in. Henry became shortstop for the Bears. His first time at bat seemed to set the stage for his career —he smashed a pitch over the left-field fence for a home run. Before long, with Henry at short and batting third, the Bears were the most exciting team in the Mobile City Recreation League. Bears fans boasted that no pitcher in the league could get Aaron out twice in a row.

Henry continued to play with the Bears, and during his third summer with them his career took a big step up towards the major leagues. For the first time, the Bears were scheduled to play a professional team—the Indianapolis Clowns of the Negro National League. This league was made up of blacks who were good enough to play professional baseball but could not play in any other league because of their color. The Indianapolis Clowns never played in Indianapolis. They picked that name because they felt a team had to be from somewhere.

Although the Bears were the best sand-lot team in the Mobile area, they did not look good in the first of their two games against Indianapolis. The Clowns walked all over the Bears on their way to a 12–2 victory. The Bears' two runs came on Henry's double with the bases loaded in the eighth inning.

But the second game on the following day was another story. In the first inning, Henry lifted a pitch over the left-field fence for a home run. Three innings later, he slashed a triple to left center, driving in two more runs. He scored on a sacrifice fly. In the sixth, he singled. Then, in the bottom half of the ninth, came his biggest hit of the game. With two men on base and the Bears trailing 9–7, Henry connected on a 3–0 pitch and knocked it over the left-field fence for the game-winning home run.

7

That same day, he was offered $200 a month to join the Clowns.

Although he spoke of nothing else to his parents, Mr. and Mrs. Aaron were not at all sure that joining the Clowns would be the best thing for their son. They were pleased that he had done so well, but they still hoped that he would go on to college. When they realized that Henry wasn't going to change his mind, however, they agreed to let him join the Indianapolis club.

In May, 1952, 18-year-old Henry Aaron boarded the first train he had ever been on in his life. He was on his way to Winston-Salem, North Carolina, where the Clowns were training. He was nervous but, at the same time, he was very excited.

Once Henry arrived at spring training, he had no time to think about anything but baseball. He was busy from early in the morning until bedtime.

The first thing he had to work on was his hitting. Although Henry was a right-hander, he batted cross-handed. The proper way for a right-hander to hold the bat is with the right hand above the left. Henry, however, held his left hand over his right. By holding his hands this way, he wasn't getting a complete follow-through. This meant that he was losing a great deal of power. There was also the chance that he could hurt his wrists. The Clowns' owner told him that he would never make the majors hitting that way.

With the quiet determination he has shown throughout his career, Henry set about correcting his swing. It wasn't easy for him to change, but with a lot of hard work Henry was soon holding the bat correctly. The result was that he had a great deal more power than before.

While he was with Indianapolis, Henry developed the batting style that he has had ever since. He stands very relaxed, far back in the batter's box. He favors a "closed stance," with his feet slightly apart and the left foot a little closer to the plate than the right. He holds the bat high above his shoulder, with his right elbow lifted up, away from his body.

During the long hours of batting practice, Henry also developed his almost perfect timing. When he sees a pitch he likes, he

At the plate, Hank Aaron prefers a closed stance.

holds his swing until the last split second. In fact, sometimes he seems to hit the ball right out of the catcher's mitt. Aaron is able to do this because he is a wrist hitter. Rather than using his arms to get power, he gets it by snapping his wrists. "I turn my wrists over," he says. "My right hand turns over toward the pitcher so, when I hit the ball, there's a rotation on it." Since he hits this way, he can connect with bad pitches as well as with good ones.

In his first time at bat for the Indianapolis team, the 5'11", 170-pound shortstop drilled a 2–0 pitch into left center for a triple, and scored on a long fly. He also singled and drew a base-on-balls. On his first day as a professional, he went 2-for-4. That was just the beginning for young Aaron, for he improved with each game he played.

It wasn't long before Henry attracted the attention of several major-league teams. The Philadelphia Phillies, the New York Giants, and the Boston Braves all sent scouts to look him over. Both the Giants and the Braves offered him a contract.

Hank gets his power by snapping his wrists as he swings at the ball.

The Braves wanted Aaron for their Class C team in Eau Claire, Wisconsin. The Giants wanted him for their Class A team. Although the C team was not as good as the A team, the Braves offered him $350 a month, $50 more than the Giants. So Henry signed with the Braves.

Because they would not pay the extra $50 a month, the Giants missed having both Henry Aaron and Willie Mays on the same team.

If the Giants had offered Aaron $50 more per month while he was with the Indianapolis Clowns, he and Willie Mays would have been teammates.

Henry finished the 1952 season with Eau Claire. It was one of the toughest periods of his life. Aside from the hard work, it was the first time he had stayed with white people. He lived alone, in a room at the YMCA.

At that time in the South, blacks and whites were segregated in many ways. Henry knew which public places were closed to him. But he had never been in the North before, and soon found that he could not go into restaurants and hotels where blacks were supposed to be welcome. He also found that some of his teammates, as well as some sports reporters, were prejudiced against him because of his color.

It was difficult for an 18-year-old to face such discrimination alone. Many times he thought about giving up and going back home to Toulmanville. But he was determined to be a major-league baseball player, and he stuck it out.

Loneliness and homesickness did not affect Aaron's playing. In 87 games with Eau Claire, he collected 9 homers and batted in 61 runs, for a .336 batting average. He was also developing speed as a base runner, and had chalked up 25 stolen bases. At the end of the season, he was the second best hitter in the Northern League, and was named Rookie of the Year.

The next season, Aaron was sent to the Braves' Class A team in Jacksonville, Florida. The team was in the South Atlantic, or "Sally," League, and Henry would be one of its first black players. He knew that being a black player with the Jacksonville Tars meant that he would face insults and discrimination. But he also knew that the move meant that the Braves' management had faith in him. He would also be a step closer to the majors. So he packed his bag and left Eau Claire for Jacksonville. The Tars already had Felix Mantilla at short, so Aaron was to play second base.

Henry found all the prejudice and resentment he had expected. On opening day of the 1953 season, the white crowd booed and jeered him as he knelt in the on-deck circle. But his powerful bat soon silenced the boos. Before the game was over, one or two people in the crowd even cheered him.

Off the field, the situation was even worse.

When Hank Aaron arrived in Jacksonville, he was
booed by white fans in the ball park. But, with the
encouragement of Manager Ben Geraghty, Hank was
able to overcome this prejudice, and soon became
the strongest hitter on the team.

Aaron, Mantilla, and Horace Garner were the first blacks on the Jacksonville team. Because of the laws of segregation, the three of them had to travel in a "split squad." They could not stay in the same hotels or eat in the same restaurants as their white teammates. Instead of going to hotels, they had to find black families who would take them into their homes as guests. Instead of going to restaurants, they had to wait for their white teammates to bring food out to them. They ate in the bus as they traveled from city to city.

It was in Jacksonville that Henry gained his nickname. The Tars were trailing 4–2 in the bottom half of the ninth in a game against Columbia, South Carolina. Aaron was up. As he waited out the windup, one of the Tars yelled, "Get ahold of one, Hank!" Aaron pulled the 1–1 pitch just inside the third-base corner for a double. The rally was on. Hank scored on a single, and the Tars went on to take the game, 5–4. After that day, his teammates always called him Hank.

Aaron ended his first season with the

While he was with the Tars, Aaron was voted the Most Valuable Player in the Sally League.

Tars as the Sally League's Most Valuable Player. His batting average was a healthy .362. He had 22 home runs, 208 hits, and 125 RBIs. He led the league in runs scored, as well as total number of hits and doubles. He was second in home runs and triples. His hitting ability had made him the Sally League player most fans went to see. But he also led the league in fielding errors, with 36.

At the close of the 1953 season, Henry married Barbara Lucas, whom he had met that year. She was a student at Florida A&M, the college his parents had hoped he would attend. Henry and Barbara went to Puerto Rico for the winter. He was to play with the Braves' farm team in the Puerto Rican League.

Hank's manager there was Mickey Owen, the great catcher, whom he had watched at Hartwell Field in Mobile. Owen had been asked by the Braves' management to show Aaron how to play the outfield. Although Aaron's hitting was beginning to make a name for him, his fielding at shortstop was not. Hank admitted that he was simply not

Playing the spring exhibition with the Braves gave rookie Aaron a chance to test his bat against major-league pitching. Manager Grimm congratulated him after one of his home runs.

able to master the double play. It was not long before he became more comfortable in the outfield than he had ever been at shortstop.

When the 1954 season opened, Aaron was supposed to play for the Braves' minorleague team in Toledo, Ohio. After a year or two there, the Braves' management felt that he would be ready for the majors. But first they wanted him to play the spring exhibition series with the Braves. That way, he could get experience batting against major-league pitchers.

On March 14, the Braves played against the New York Yankees. Braves left fielder Bobby Thomson got a hit, and slid into second base trying to stretch it into a double. The umpire called him safe, but he did not get up. The trainer ran out onto the field and examined him. He found that Thomson had broken his ankle and would be out of the line-up for most of the season. Who would replace Thomson? Who would be in left field on opening day?

To the amazement of baseball writers, team players, and most of all Henry him-

A bad break for Braves' outfielder Bobby Thomson turned out to be the luckiest break of Aaron's career. Trained to play outfield in Puerto Rico, Hank was ready to replace the veteran after his accident.

self, manager Charlie Grimm picked young Aaron to fill in for the veteran Thomson. When the Braves opened their second season in Milwaukee (the team had been moved from Boston), Henry Aaron was their regular left fielder. He later explained it by saying, "All the breaks came my way that spring. Because I had played winter ball to get outfield experience, I was in tiptop shape for playing."

The rookie left fielder's first few games showed that he still had a lot to learn. He couldn't get a hit and he made serious fielding errors. In one game, his cap fell off while he was rounding the bases, and he went back to get it! That was one of the most serious mistakes he made.

But manager Grimm had faith that Hank would develop into an outstanding ballplayer. He knew that Aaron's main problem was that he was trying too hard.

Finally, on April 23, Grimm's faith and Hank's hard work paid off. Aaron hit his first major-league home run off St. Louis Cardinals pitcher Vic Raschi. After that, Hank began to play major-league baseball.

That season, the Milwaukee team played the kind of heads-up baseball that spells winners. They were pressing close on the heels of the league-leading Brooklyn Dodgers. Their attack was led by Aaron's relentless pounding of the National League's hurlers.

By the end of May, Hank's bat had hammered a place for him as Milwaukee's cleanup hitter. Coming up fourth, he would have more chance to drive in runs, since one or more of the first three men up were likely to get on base.

Sparked by Hank's bat, the Braves held their own as they challenged the Dodgers. Then they moved ahead to take over first place. But the pressure on the rookie was too much, and Aaron went into a slump. Without Hank to fire them, the Braves dropped into second place. Then the New York Giants took off on a winning streak that lifted them to first place and pushed the Braves into third. But Milwaukee was still very much in the picture, especially after Aaron began to hammer his way out of his slump in late August.

On September 5, Hank was having a good day. He had hit a double, a homer, and a triple, and the Braves led the Cubs, 9–2. At bat in the ninth inning, Hank found a pitch he liked and drilled it into left center. He rounded second and headed for third. It was going to be a close play. He slid. The umpire called the play—safe! But Hank had broken his ankle.

Bobby Thomson's ankle had just healed, so he took over in left field for the rest of the season. The Braves finished third, but Hank's spot in the regular line-up was assured.

During the winter, Hank spent a lot of time working with children in Mobile, teaching them about baseball. He felt at ease with young people, sharing his experiences, talking to them, and answering their questions.

That winter, to keep in shape, Aaron also played basketball and baseball with local teams. He also worked on his weaknesses. He remembers, "Don Drysdale used to get me out with the change of pace pitch. In fact, *all* of the Dodgers used to kill me with that pitch. So, after my first year, when I got home to Mobile, I'd get my brother Tommy to throw change-ups to me all the time."

When he reported for spring training, he was feeling fine—and he had become a father for the first time.

In 1955, his first full season with the Braves, Henry Aaron was still very quiet and soft-spoken. He did not brag about what he could do or try to get attention for himself. Instead, as he always had, he let his bat speak for him. "I just went out and did the best I could," he said. "I'm no chit-chat guy."

Aaron was not only a sensational hitter, he was dependable as well. More important, he was an outstanding team player. He was not looking for glory for himself. Rather, he wanted the Braves to win a pennant.

Milwaukee didn't win the pennant that year, though they finished in second place, 13½ games behind the Dodgers. Hank had a season's average of .314, with 27 home runs, 106 RBIs, and 105 runs scored.

1955 was also a memorable year in other

Hank Aaron won the 1956 National League batting championship. Warren Giles, League president, presented him with a silver bat to commemorate his achievement.

ways. For the first time, he was chosen to play in the All-Star game. The Milwaukee baseball writers named him the Most Valuable Brave, and he won the National League batting championship in 1956. But in spite of his personal honors, the Braves still ran second to the Dodgers.

When the Braves played poorly early in 1956, Charley Grimm was replaced as manager by Fred Haney. Hank also began the season in a slump. Then suddenly he caught fire and hit in 25 straight games. By the 1957 season, National League pitchers were asking each other what the "book" was on Aaron—what his weaknesses were. In return, Aaron said, "I keep a mental book on what pitchers throw me. When I'm hitting well, I can tell what a pitch will be when it's halfway to the plate."

Dodger Roy Campanella described Hank as the best right-handed hitter he had ever seen. Led by Aaron's bat, the Braves fought their way into first place, a half game ahead of the St. Louis Cardinals.

Then, one day in July, just when things were going better than ever for the Braves,

Hank sprained his ankle trying to stretch a double into a triple. The Braves' trainer said that he would be sidelined for two weeks. Although Hank wanted to go on playing, he knew the ankle would get worse if he did. So he went home to Mobile to wait for it to heal.

For some time, Henry and Barbara Aaron had been talking about buying a home and settling down in Milwaukee. Their family was growing, with two children, Gaile and Henry, Jr., and another on the way. They saw the house they wanted, but it was in an all-white neighborhood. The Aarons were not sure whether they would be made welcome there. Nevertheless, while Hank was recovering from his injury, they decided to make the move.

Once again, Hank discovered that his bat meant more than the color of his skin. The children in their new neighborhood followed him around, asking his advice on batting and fielding. Their parents, too, often spoke with him about baseball and the team.

While the Aarons were busy moving into their new home, the Braves had taken off on a losing streak. Without Hank in the line-up, they couldn't win a game.

Eight days after his injury, Hank returned for a game with the Dodgers. His ankle was still swollen, so the trainer taped it tightly. Manager Fred Haney didn't want Aaron to play, but Hank was determined. When his name was announced, batting in the cleanup slot, cheers thundered through County Stadium.

The Braves and Dodgers had battled to a 6-all deadlock as Hank came up in the bottom half of the ninth. There were two out and two men on base. Aaron worked the count to 2–2, fouling off the first pitch, passing up two bad ones, and taking a called strike two. Then Dodger relief pitcher Clem Labine delivered one Hank liked. He cracked the ball into the stands for the game-winning home run.

For the next few days, Hank played with a taped ankle. But what mattered was that he was back in the line-up. The Braves had been losing while he was laid up. With his bat back, the team caught fire again. They took the next 10 straight games and were leading the league at the end of August.

After a losing streak in early September, the Braves opened a four-game series against the second-place Cardinals. The Milwaukee team needed just one win to take the pennant.

County Stadium was packed solid for the series opener. Every hit brought the screaming fans to their feet as the two teams battled for 10½ innings to a 2–2 tie. Then Hank came up to face Cards pitcher Larry Jackson, with two out and one on.

When Aaron stepped up to the plate, the crowd began to clap in rhythm. "We want a hit! We want a hit!" Hank knocked the dirt from his cleats and dug in. "We want a hit! We want a HIT!" thundered from the stands.

As Jackson glanced over his shoulder to check on Red Schoendienst leading off second, the clapping and stamping became deafening. Waiting for Jackson, Aaron stood in the batter's box relaxed and unmoving. Jackson stretched and delivered. Hank hit the ball, and there was no doubt

Aaron's 11th inning home run brought the Braves their first pennant.

where it was heading. The fans went wild. Once again, Hank Aaron came through in the clutch! The Braves had brought Milwaukee its first National League flag.

The entire team greeted Hank when he jumped on home plate with both feet. They shook his hand, pounded his back, and carried him off the field on their shoulders.

33

But there was still the World Series to be played. The Braves would be facing the team that had been winning the World Series for years—the New York Yankees.

New York took the first game of the series. The next day, the Braves evened it up. The Yankees took the third game; the Braves claimed the fourth and the fifth. In the sixth game, the Yankees tied the series.

The Yankees were favored to take the seventh game and the series. But the Braves would not give up. They clobbered the Yankee pitching staff for a 5–0 win—and were world champions!

During the series, Hank hit safely 11 times, including 3 homers, and batted in 7 runs.

His batting average for the year was .322. He had 44 home runs and 132 RBIs. Aaron explained his performance by saying, "I just leave the dugout swinging. The secret of hitting is to keep swinging." The Baseball Writers' Association named him the Most Valuable Player in the National League for 1957.

Yankee hurler Tom Sturdivant (42) served up a perfect pitch to Hank Aaron in the fourth game of the World Series. Aaron turned it into a 3-run homer.

In October, Hank returned to Mobile to visit his parents. He was greeted by 2,000 fans, and Mobile's Mayor Joseph Langan presented him with a gold "key to the city." To top it off, the Mayor proclaimed the day "Hank Aaron Day."

Two months later, Barbara Aaron gave birth to twin boys whom she and Hank named Gary and Larry. But two days after he was born, Gary died.

Hank was still upset over the baby's death when the 1958 season began. He had always been able to leave his troubles behind when he went on the field, but not this time. By the last week in June, he was batting only .254. With a weak-hitting Aaron, the championship Braves fell apart.

Then, one day in a game against the Giants, Hank singled his last two times at bat. In his next 11 at-bats, he got 9 hits. His slump was over. Before long, he was over .300 again. During July, his average zoomed up almost 80 points. Asked about his comeback, he shrugged and said, "You swing the bat. Sometimes you hit the ball; sometimes you don't."

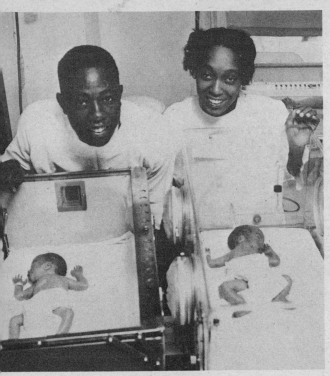

In December, 1957, the Aarons became the proud parents of twin boys, Larry and Gary. But Gary only lived for two days.

Hammerin' Hank became Hustlin' Hank when he scored from first on a single in a game against the Cincinnati Reds. Reds' catcher Dutch Dotterer tried to block the plate. But Aaron's hook slide got him past and home safe.

A bunt by Aaron is truly a rare sight. This one caught the Giants' infield flat-footed and was good for a single. (1960)

The Braves were back in the pennant race, going ahead of the San Francisco Giants to lead the league.

Again the season's deciding game was played in County Stadium, this time against Cincinnati. The Redlegs were ahead, 5–4, when Hank came up to bat in the seventh inning. Eddie Mathews was on first, so a homer could mean the ballgame and the pennant. Once again, Aaron came through. He belted the home run that brought Milwaukee its second flag.

The World Series was between the Yankees and the Braves for the second year in a row. And although Hank batted .333 during the series, the Yankees won.

The following season—1959—was one of the best of Hank's career. His .355 average led the league. He hit 39 home runs, batted in 113 runs, and boasted a hitting streak of 22 games. During that season, he connected for the 1,000th hit of his career. National League players and sports writers began to compare him to baseball's finest sluggers—Ted Williams, Mickey Mantle, Stan Musial, and Willie Mays. Some even said that Hank Aaron would be the greatest of them all.

The season ended in a first-place tie between the Braves and the Dodgers, who were now in Los Angeles. In the play-off games that followed, the Braves dropped two straight, and the Dodgers took the pennant.

The Braves team began to lose steadily after that. In the years that followed, players were traded to build up the team's batting and pitching. One manager after another was hired and then fired. No matter what moves they made, the Braves were going nowhere. They dropped to fourth, finished third three times, and then fell to sixth place.

All this time, Hank Aaron hit regularly over .300 and averaged over 40 home runs in a season.

In 1966, the Braves left Milwaukee for a new home. They were now playing in Braves Stadium, Atlanta, Georgia. Again, Aaron was afraid that he and his family would face discrimination. But Atlanta fans were thrilled to have their own base-

Milwaukee's Hank Aaron (44) strides across home
plate after hitting a grand slam home run into the
left centerfield bleachers of New York's Polo Grounds
in a game with the New York Mets on June 18, 1962.
The blow was Aaron's second 4-run homer in four
days and the first to clear the ball park's left center-
field wall since Joe Adcock of the Braves belted a
ball into the area in 1953. Braves scoring ahead
of Aaron were Eddie Matthews (41), Del Crandall
(1), and Roy McMillan (11). Mets' catcher Sammy
Taylor (16) is at left and Milwaukee's next batter,
Gus Bell, is number 20. The Braves won, 7-1.

ball team. They were even more thrilled to have a slugger like Hank Aaron on that team. They made him and his family feel welcome.

In spite of a spectacular effort by Aaron, this one got away. (1963)

Hank Aaron was one of the most popular players in the annual Jimmy Fund Game. The game was played each year between the Braves and the Boston Red Sox. The proceeds were used for research on cancer in children. (1966)

Off to visit American troops in Vietnam are Stan Musial, Joe Torres, Hank Aaron, Harmon Killebrew and Brooks Robinson.

During the winter of 1966, Hank and a group of baseball stars visited American soldiers in Vietnam. On his return, Hank signed a two-year contract with the Braves, which gave him a salary of $100,000 a year. Baseball fans and sports writers still did not think of Aaron as a superstar. But he knew he was, and the Braves' management knew it, too. So they agreed that he was worth a superstar's salary.

46

While the Braves were playing their way into a disappointing seventh place in 1967, Hank batted in the 1,500th run of his career. One year later, he hit a 400-foot blast off Mike McCormick of the Giants for his 500th home run. Dodger strike-out ace Sandy Koufax called him the toughest batter in the league and complained, "There's no way to pitch to him when he's hot!"

But Aaron says, "Consistency is what counts. You have to be able to do things over and over again."

By 1969, Hank was in seventh place on the all-time home run list. That year, he hammered his way up to third. His 44 round-trippers took him past Mel Ott, Eddie Mathews, Ted Williams, Jimmy Foxx, and Mickey Mantle. By the end of the season, only Willie Mays and Babe Ruth were ahead of him.

The Braves came back to life in '69. By now, the National League had expanded to 12 teams, which were divided into the Eastern Division and Western Division. The Braves were in the Western Division, and they won its pennant. But under the new league rules, they still had to play the Eastern Division winner to get to the World Series. The Braves faced the amazing New York Mets in the three-game play-off. Hank hit two doubles and three homers and drove in seven runs. But in spite of his performance, the Mets took all three games.

The 1970 season was not a good one for the Braves. Hank, however, went on playing as he always had. On May 17, he reached his 3,000th hit. Some sports writers began to hint that Hank would soon slow down. He was 36 years old, which is considered old for a baseball player.

The next year, Hank's .327 average included 118 RBIs. It also included 47 home runs, the most he had ever hit in one season. One of the home runs was at the expense of Gaylord Perry, the San Francisco Giants' ace pitcher. Perry had been talking with newspaper reporters before the game when the subject of Aaron and his home runs came up. Someone commented that Hank was one away from 600, and Perry said, "If he gets it off me, he's going to earn it!"

Aaron leaps high and crashes into the rightfield wall to rob the Giants' Dick Dietz of a 3-run homer.

Aaron loses his protective helmet as he ducks a
close pitch during the 1969 Braves-Mets playoff
series. The Braves lost all three games to the Mets.

On May 16, 1970, Henry Aaron connected for the 3,000th hit of his major-league career.

Hammerin' Hank lifted his 600th home run in Atlanta Stadium on April 28, 1971. San Francisco Giants' pitcher Gaylord Perry was his victim.

At 36, which is old for a baseball player, Aaron was still stealing bases. Here, Hank stole second and was safe. Mets' shortstop Bud Harelson sprawled on the ground after missing a wild toss from pitcher Tom Seaver. Aaron moved to third on the error.

Aaron appeared with Horace Davis, executive director of the Black Athletes' Foundation for Sickle Cell Anemia, before the Senate Subcommittee on Health.

After the game, Hank was told about Perry's remark. He laughed and said, "I guess I earned it."

Between seasons, Hank spent a good deal of his time working with children, teaching them baseball and basketball. He was also an active member of the Black Athletes' Foundation for Sickle Cell Anemia, and he appeared before the Senate Subcommittee on Health. The athletes wanted the federal government to set aside money for research on the disease, which strikes one out of every 10 black people and is very often fatal.

"Many times we black athletes haven't spoken out," Aaron said. "I've been guilty myself. But I've learned that when you don't say anything, people think you are satisfied."

The quiet kid from Toulmanville became the highest-paid player in baseball history in 1972. Hank was now earning $200,000 a year.

In 1972, Braves president Bill Bartholomay offered Aaron a contract that made him the highest-paid player in baseball history. Hank was now earning $200,000 a year. Bartholomay said, "He deserves every penny of it."

On the last day of May, Hank hit a 3–2 pitch from San Diego's Fred Norman for his 648th home run, tying Willie Mays on the all-time homer list. Ten days later, with the bases loaded, Philadelphia Phils hurler Wayne Twitchell tried to sneak a fast ball past the Braves' slugger. Aaron snapped his wrists, and Twitchell watched the ball clear the left-field wall. Hank passed Mays on the list by hitting the 14th grand slam of his career. It also tied him with Gil Hodges for most grand slams by a National League batter.

Now there was only one man in baseball who had hit more home runs—Babe Ruth.

By season's end, Hank had driven in over 2,000 runs, had chalked up 1,300 extra-base hits, and had a record-breaking 6,177 total bases to his credit. More important,

When Aaron passed Willie Mays on the all-time home run list, only one player in baseball history had hit more home runs than he—Babe Ruth.

he ended the baseball year with 34 home
runs for a lifetime total of 673. Sports writers began to talk about Hank and the greatest record of all—Babe Ruth's lifetime
record of 714 home runs.

Many people were surprised to learn that
Hank was so close to breaking that record.
How could it possibly have happened?
Hank was not a player they had been hear-
ing much about. But when they checked
the records, they discovered that for his 19
seasons in the majors, Aaron had averaged

On September 3, 1972, Aaron became the all-time
major-league leader in total bases. That day, he got
the 6,135th of his career, to put him one ahead of
Stan Musial.

35 homers each year. Hank Aaron was, indeed, challenging Babe Ruth's home run record.

But Hank was now 39 years old. Could he keep up his steady pace? Could he hit 42 more homers? Could he really break Babe Ruth's record?

On April 6, 1973, the Braves met the Houston Astros for the opening night game of the season. All eyes were on Hank Aaron. His battle to top Ruth's record had begun.

But as the season wore on, breaking the record was only part of the struggle Aaron had to face. There were many people who did not want Ruth's record broken—and especially not by a black man. The closer Hank came to the record, the more hate mail he received.

In many of the letters, he was called names. In others, his life was threatened. Even worse than the letters were the insults shouted at him while he was playing. One man made Hank so angry that he lost his temper on the field for the first time in his career.

In spite of threats and hate mail, Aaron continued to close in on Babe Ruth's record. His parents, Mr. and Mrs. Herbert Aaron, were among his most enthusiastic supporters.

Hank was determined not to let these people stop him. He explained: "Because of the position I'm in, I hope I can inspire a few kids to be a success in life. I want to break Ruth's record as an example to children, especially black children. I consider myself a baseball player first and a black man second—and I'm proud of both."

Aaron was given extra protection when the team was on the road, and he was carefully guarded at home. To add to his troubles, his marriage had not been going well. He and Barbara decided to get a divorce. For the first time in his life, the shy, quiet Henry Aaron was "news" to sports writers.

He found himself answering the same questions over and over again. Usually he laughed when he was asked about Ruth's record. But sometimes he became angry. Then the sports writers who had ignored him for so long said that the pressure was getting to him and that, because of it, he might not be able to break Ruth's record.

With all his problems that season, Hank still played much as he always had. But because he was older and tired more quick-

During the 1973 season, Aaron began to play the infield once more. Playing first base was easier on his legs than chasing flies in the outfield.

Hank acknowledges the crowd's cheers after hitting #700.

ly, he missed more games than usual, sitting out some to rest. He played the infield more because it would be easier on his legs. But his bat was as strong as ever.

On July 8, Hank hit homers 695 and 696 against the Mets. Thirteen days later he clouted #700, and the crowd of nearly 20,000 gave him a two-minute standing ovation.

In August, Aaron connected for homers 702 to 708. He got two in a game against the San Diego Padres. On September 10, he hit the 710th of his career. On September 17, he made it 711 on an eighth-inning, 0–1 pitch from Gary Ross of the Padres.

There were two men on when Aaron came up in the fifth inning on September 29. Jerry Reuss of the Houston Astros served up a slow curve ball around the knees. Hank slammed a high drive over the left center-field wall of Atlanta Stadium. The ball hit against the message board at the same moment that "713" flashed on the board in lights. Hank was now one short of Ruth's record.

... #707 (and #708 in the same game)

On the last day of the 1973 season, 40,517 spectators poured into Atlanta Stadium. Hank was not served any home run pitches that day, but he did get three singles.

When Hank trotted out to his position in left field in the first half of the ninth, cheers began in the left-field stands. The roar moved around the stadium, until all the people were on their feet—clapping, stomping, and cheering. The game was stopped as the cheering continued. Every so often, Hank waved to the fans. After three minutes, the game was started again, but the fans wouldn't stop.

Throughout the following winter, Hank Aaron's name was heard everywhere. Everyone knew he would break Ruth's record. It was just a matter of when.

Two months before the opening day of the 1974 season, a new storm broke with Hank at its center. The Braves were to open in Cincinnati. Braves' Chairman Bill Bartholomay wanted to bench his superstar until the team's first game in Atlanta.

71

#713. Hank Aaron ended the 1973 season needing one home run to tie Ruth's record and two to break it.

On the closing day of the 1973 season, Aaron was
given a standing ovation by more than 40,000 fans.

But sports writers and baseball fans argued that Aaron *should* play against Cincinnati.

Finally, in mid-March, Baseball Commissioner Bowie Kuhn stepped in. He said, "Barring disability, I will expect the Braves to use Henry Aaron in Cincinnati . . ."

Commissioner Kuhn was among the 52,154 fans in Riverfront Stadium on Thursday afternoon, April 4, when the Braves met the Reds in the opener. Six minutes after the game started, with two men on, Hank blasted a 3–1 sinker served up by Reds pitcher, Jack Billingham. The ball cleared the left-field fence 377 feet from the plate. The record was tied.

The next day, the Braves were idle. On Saturday, Aaron was benched. Again, the Commissioner stepped in. Aaron was to play on Sunday, he said. Aaron played, but went hitless.

On April 8, 1974, the Braves opened their home season with a game against the Los Angeles Dodgers. 53,775 excited fans crowded into Atlanta Stadium to see if Henry Aaron would make baseball history that night.

In November, 1973, Hank married Billye Williams in Kingston, Jamaica.

The first pitch to Hank was high for a ball. Dodgers pitcher Al Downing wasn't going to give the Braves slugger anything too good. The crowd booed. The second pitch was a called strike. This time the boos were for the plate umpire. Ball two in the dirt brought more boos. A low ball three and the boos were louder still. When Aaron walked on an outside pitch, the fans yelled their protest.

Hank came up again in the fourth, and the first pitch was in the dirt. The boos started again. Then Downing threw a fast ball, right down the middle. It was 9:07 P.M. when it happened. Looking as relaxed as ever, Aaron snapped his wrists. The ball met the bat with a crack that could be heard throughout Atlanta Stadium. As the crowd screamed and cheered, the ball soared towards left-center. It cleared the fence near the 385-foot sign and landed in the Braves' bullpen. It was Aaron's first swing of the game and his 715th home run.

As he rounded the bases, skyrockets were fired and "715" appeared in lights on the scoreboard. The crowd thundered a wild

Aaron's eyes were on the ball as he made baseball history.

ovation. Hank's teammates and his parents rushed to home plate to congratulate him.

What was he thinking about after becoming the greatest home-run hitter of all time?

"I just wanted to touch all the bases," said Aaron.

Hank had said that he would retire at the end of the 1974 season. His future plans though were uncertain. There was the possibility that he might become the first black manager of a major-league team. Half-way through the season, the Braves had begun looking for a new manager. The job was not offered to Hank. He was very upset, and said so. Because of this, there was a question about his staying in baseball.

At the end of the season, Hank was traded to the Milwaukee Brewers as a Designated Hitter. He was delighted to be returning to Milwaukee. However, he had to abandon his hope of being the first black manager. That all-time honor went to Frank Robinson of the Cleveland Indians.

During the 1974 season, Hank added another record to his impressive list. This

The Braves congratulate their teammate at home plate after he set the new record.

one: Most Grand Slams, National League. His 16th career grand slam, which was also his 723rd homer, came on June 4, and broke the record of Willie McCovey of San Diego. Lou Gehrig still holds the major-league record of 23 grand slams.

Early in the next season, Aaron broke another Babe Ruth record—the most career RBIs. Officials differ about whether Ruth had 2,199 RBIs or 2,209. But on May 2, 1975, in a game against the Detroit Tigers, Hank drilled a single down the left-field line to score teammate, Sixto Lezcano, for his 2,210th RBI. By any standard, the record was his.

But his most important record is still: most home runs, career—Henry Louis Aaron.

APPENDIX

HENRY LOUIS (HANK) AARON

Born February 5, 1934, at Mobile, Ala.

Height, 6.00. Weight, 180.   Bats and throws righthanded.

BATTING RECORD

Year Club	P	G	AB	R	H	TB	2B	3B	HR	RBI	Pct.
1952 Eau Claire	SS	87	345	79	116	170	19	4	9	61	.336
1953 Jacksonville	2B	137	574	115	208	338	36	14	22	125	.362
1954 Milwaukee	OF	122	468	58	131	209	27	6	13	69	.280
1955 Milwaukee	OF-2B	153	602	105	189	325	37	9	27	106	.314
1956 Milwaukee	OF	153	609	106	200	340	34	14	26	92	.328
1957 Milwaukee	OF	151	615	118	198	369	27	6	44	132	.322
1958 Milwaukee	OF	153	601	109	196	328	34	4	30	95	.326
1959 Milwaukee	OF-3B	154	629	116	223	400	46	7	39	123	.355
1960 Milwaukee	OF-2B	153	590	102	172	334	20	11	40	126	.292
1961 Milwaukee	OF-3B	155	603	115	197	358	39	10	34	120	.327
1962 Milwaukee	OF-1B	156	592	127	191	366	28	6	45	128	.323
1963 Milwaukee	OF	161	631	121	201	370	29	4	44	130	.319
1964 Milwaukee	OF-2B	145	570	103	187	293	30	2	24	95	.328

Year	Team	Pos	G	AB	R	H	TB	2B	3B	HR	RBI	Pct.
1965	Milwaukee	OF	150	570	109	181	319	40	1	32	89	.318
1966	Atlanta	OF-2B	158	603	117	168	325	23	1	44	127	.279
1967	Atlanta	OF-2B	155	600	113	184	344	37	3	39	109	.307
1968	Atlanta	OF-1B	160	606	84	174	302	33	4	29	86	.287
1969	Atlanta	OF-1B	147	547	100	164	332	30	3	44	97	.300
1970	Atlanta	OF-1B	150	516	103	154	296	26	1	38	118	.298
1971	Atlanta	1B-OF	139	495	95	162	331	22	3	47	118	.327
1972	Atlanta	1B-OF	129	449	75	119	231	10	0	34	77	.265
1973	Atlanta	OF	120	392	84	118	252	12	1	40	96	.301
1974	Milwaukee (Brewers)	OF	112	340	47	91	167	16	0	20	69	.268
Major League Totals		.3076	11628	2107	3600	6591	600	96	733	2202	.310

WORLD SERIES RECORD

	G	AB	R	H	TB	2B	3B	HR	RBI	Pct.
1957 Milwaukee vs New York	7	28	5	11	22	0	1	3	7	.393
1958 Milwaukee vs New York	7	27	3	9	11	2	0	0	2	.333
World Series Totals	14	55	8	20	33	2	1	3	9	.364

29557 JOHNNY/BINGO, by Browning Norton. Kidnapped by ruthless bank robbers, two thirteen-year-old boys carry out a bold plan of escape. (75¢)

29523 THE TERRIBLE CHURNADRYNE, by Eleanor Cameron. Illustrated by Beth and Joe Krush. A strange and terrifying creature stalks Jennifer and Tom as they are returning home through the fog at dusk. (75¢)

29767 ENCYCLOPEDIA BROWN SHOWS THE WAY, by Donald J. Sobol. Illustrated by Leonard Shortall. Join the famous Encyclopedia Brown in ten more challenging cases as he discovers the clues needed to catch Idaville's sneakiest criminals. (95¢)

29765 THREE ON THE RUN, by Nina Bawden. Frontispiece illustration by Wendy Worth. Sudden adventure grips Ben, Lil, and their African friend, Thomas Okapi, as they are plunged into an international plot and must make a wild, desperate flight from London. ($1.25)

29707 JACKIE ROBINSON OF THE BROOKLYN DODGERS, by Milton J. Shapiro. Illustrated with photographs. The courageous black man who broke the color line in professional baseball and became one of the all-time greats of the Brooklyn Dodgers. (95¢)

29546 DRUGS AND YOU, by Arnold Madison. Illustrated with photographs. This straightforward account gives you basic information about the use and abuse of today's major drugs. (75¢)

29526 ALVIN FERNALD, FOREIGN TRADER, by Clifford B. Hicks. Illustrated by Bill Sokol. Alvin goes on a glorious but zany trip to Europe and gets involved with industrial spies. (75¢)

29770 PERPLEXING PUZZLES AND TANTALIZING TEASERS, by Martin Gardner. Illustrated by Laszlo Kubinyi. A fascinating collection of puzzles and teasers to challenge your wits, tickle your funny bone, and give you and your friends hours of entertainment. (95¢)

29311 LITTLE VIC, by Doris Gates. Illustrated by Kate Seredy. A young man's courageous struggle to qualify as a jockey and to ride the horse he loves to victory. (60¢)

29566 WHITE WATER, STILL WATER, by J. Allan Bosworth. Illustrated by Charles W. Walker. Swept down river on a raft, Chris faces a hazardous journey home through the wilderness— barefoot and equipped with nothing but a broken-bladed pocketknife. (75¢)

29750